Anonymous

Fishing

When, Where, and How to Fish Without Live Bait

Anonymous

Fishing
When, Where, and How to Fish Without Live Bait

ISBN/EAN: 9783744679404

Printed in Europe, USA, Canada, Australia, Japan

Cover: Foto ©Andreas Hilbeck / pixelio.de

More available books at **www.hansebooks.com**

FISHING:

WHEN, WHERE, AND HOW

TO

FISH WITHOUT LIVE BAIT.

LONDON:
WILLIAM TWEEDIE, 337, STRAND.

1862.

INTRODUCTION.

NOTHING will make you a good angler but observation, practice, and experience. You must *see* fishing; you must yourself *fish;* and you must *learn by both.* Careful practice only will make you master of the art. A few general hints may help you. Here they are ;—first upon

THE ROD.

This you may make for yourself, or it may be bought, cheap, ready-made. Begin with a light one. It should be supple, and bend uniformly like an arch. If it bends sharply at an angle, a stout fish will break it at the angle. A few straight hazel rods, cut from the hedge, of different sizes, so as to taper regularly, and made to fit into tin ferules, will do to begin with; or it may be made of bamboo. The best rods are made of hickory; but they are for large fish, and are expensive. Provide yourself with two or three top pieces, as they are liable to break. Have but few rings on the rod for the line to pass through. And, for most of the small fish, a winch or reel at the foot of the rod, to wind the line upon, is quite unnecessary. A little forked stick to thrust into the ground, with the forked part upwards to rest the rod upon, when fishing for some sorts of fish, will be of great assistance, and will enable you to retire out of sight. When in shallow, clear streams, you will be more likely to get a bite.

THE LINE

You may also make for yourself, but it is better to buy it. A horse-hair ready-made line is the best for general purposes. We remember a little boy wanted to make a line for himself, who went to a stable where large white cart-horses were kept. He began to pull the long hair from their tails, when one of them kicked

him in the head. His father and mother cried very
much, and the doctors did all they could to save him,
but he died the next day, and instead of fishing through
the beautiful summer, he was carried away and buried
in the cold grave. Next to horse-hair a good silk one
will be useful. For very small fish, a line entirely of
"gut" will be found very successful. Lines are best
of a light colour.

BAIT

We have spoken of, under the name of each fish. We
may mention as a fact, that we have seen large numbers
of roach and dace pulled out of the Thames with a little
bit of white kid glove on the hook instead of a fly.
The angler was "fly-fishing," that is, throwing his line
as though he had a fly on the hook, when the fish
bit at every two or three throws, and he pulled out
more than a hundred in a very short time. Try for
yourself.

LANDING NET.

Just the sort of little net with which the boys catch
minnows will do. But this is only necessary if you

hook a large fish, which by the way, is sometimes done when fishing for small ones. When you have a large fish on the hook, do not try to pull it out of the water at once, or it will resist and break the line, and go off with the hook in it; you will thus lose line and fish. Keep a slight *strain* upon the line, and bring the fish gradually to the side, where you can put your net under it, and thus land it.

HOW TO GET THE HOOK OUT.

Many fish will drop off the hook on being brought out of the water. Generally they are hooked in the mouth or throat when that is the case—the forefinger passed down the tightened line till it presses against the bend of the hook, and then *a slight pressure further* will disengage the hook, and it may be brought away from the fish.

FISHING.

Fishing will at least teach you patience and perseverance, and "if at first you don't succeed," to catch fish, you must "try, try, and try again." After all your care and waiting, very much depends upon the *hunger* of the fish as to their "biting"—

> "If they will, they will, depend on't,
> And if they won't they won't, and there's an end on't;"

or there might as well be an end of it just at that time, or in that place.

As to bait, we, of course, shall protest strongly against the use of "live" bait: to thread a *living* worm on a hook, or to pass a hook through the body of a *living* fish, as bait, is to us a piece of cruelty which we hope none of our readers will be guilty of; if we thought they would, we should not write another line. "Live" bait is not justified by the pleasure of angling; besides, it is quite *unnecessary*, for fish can be taken nearly as well, *sometimes better*, with a bait that has no life in it.

In describing the different sorts of fish which frequent our rivers and lakes, we of course begin with the salmon.

SALMON.

The salmon holds the first place among our river fish. His beauty is unsurpassed. The salmon spawn in the months of September and October, when they may be seen passing up the river in large numbers—some say often at the rate of twenty miles an hour—to find shallow places to lay their eggs in. As they go up they will spring over "falls of water" seven and ten feet high!

June, July, and August is the best time to take salmon, when they are in fine condition, having come up from the sea, where they fatten fast in the salt water. The rivers in Ireland and Scotland are the best places for salmon, where they are taken in abundance. We have known Irish salmon sent over in long boxes, packed in ice, to Bristol, sold at 4d. and 6d. a pound. The best salmon we have tasted is the Severn. The fishermen catch them in nets on the Wye, which runs into the Severn.

The proper way for the angler to catch salmon is with an artificial fly, that is, a fly made of feathers, wool, leather, silk, &c., to look like a real fly; but you little folk can hardly expect to catch these large fish, although a gentleman tells us he once saw a shepherd boy in Peebleshire kill a prime salmon, of twelve pounds weight, with a common hazel rod and an extraordinary hair-line, without a reel or winch of any kind upon it, and with a fly exactly like a large humble bee. He hooked the fish in the deep part of the long stream, and had the sagacity and promptitude of action to throw his rod immediately into the water after the rushing and powerful fish. The force of the current took it down to the calmer end of the stream, where the stripling caught hold of it again and instantly succeeded in running the salmon into the next stream, and so on, till he had artfully exhausted his capture, and forced him into a shallow part of the water. Here he got him stranded with great adroitness, and eventually conquered him in capital style.

PIKE OR JACK.

The Pike is a strong fish and may be called the wolf of the water. They sometimes grow to a great

size and live a long time. There is a story told
—apparently upon good authority, though we think
there must be some exaggeration—that in 1497, a
person caught, near Nannheim, a pike which was
nineteen feet long, and which weighed three hundred
and fifty pounds. His skeleton was preserved for a
long time at Mannheim. He carried round his neck
a ring of gilded brass, which had been attached to
him by order of the Emperor Frederick Barbarossa,
two hundred and sixty seven years before !

You may catch pike by *trolling*, which is the
best way. A fine, fresh-caught roach put into sweet
bran will soon get firm and stiff—that is the best
bait. Do not brush the roach, because you will
rub away the scales. As soon as the hook is thrown
into the water, off goes the bran, and the fish
sparkles and glitters, with his skin whole.

A long, double-headed hook, with a leaded shank,
is thrust by a proper needle through the mouth of
the fish along in the direction of the back-bone, and

out at the tail, where it is tied with a piece of
thread ; the line, which should be fifty yards long,
is made fast to the loop at the end of the hook-
shank, and, with the help of a good stiff, shortish
rod, ten feet long, the bait is thrown as far as you
can from you ; it is then drawn through the water,
and the pike will spring at it, just as a cat does at
a mouse, seize it in its large jaws, and run off with
it to its lurking-place, and in about ten minutes
will have swallowed it ; he is then fairly hooked, and
you may "land" him if you can. If the bait is
small, he will swallow it at the time he seizes it ;
then, if not very large, you may pull him out at
once, which we have done *on the instant* of his
seizing the bait.

The boys in Huntingdonshire and Cambridgeshire
snare pike in the small streams and large ditches and
drains in those countries. A strong, stiff rod, ten
feet long, is generally used, at the end of which is a
piece of copper wire, *previously burnt in hay* to make

it pliable. A *noose* in the wire is carefully slipped over the head of the pike as he basks in the water, a sudden jerk catches him, and he is pulled out by main force.

TROUT

The trout is a very beautiful fish, and abundant in nearly all our English, Scotch, and Irish rivers. It is a fish fairly within the reach of a boy. Mr. Robert Blakey, who is the best writer we know on angling, says on fly-fishing what we think is specially applicable to this mode of fishing for trout : "It is graceful and gentlemanly, and can be enjoyed by all who exhibit any anxiety to acquire the art. It is also the most independent mode. You take your rod, fishing-reel, and fly-hook, and roam away over half a kingdom, without any further trouble about baits, or incumbrance from nets, or fish-kettles, or other trumpery. In point of exciting the mind, and sustaining joyous hilarity, it is infinitely preferable to all other modes of exercising the gentle art. The constant attention which the angler must pay to his flies as they glide on the water, the repeated changes of locality, the calm and placid pleasure infused into the soul by sparkling and gushing streams, the constant exercise of his skill in casting and drawing the line, the gentle tantalisings of his hopes by frequent unsuccessful risings at the fly, the dexterity and management requsite in killing a fish with such delicate materials, and the uncertainty which always hangs over his successful capture,—all tend to awaken and keep alive that feeling of mind on which rests the whole charm of the art. In short, in fly-fishing all the elements are judiciously combined, which contribute to render angling an agreeable and healthy amusement. . . . . . We have long arrived at the conclusion that anglers are vastly more fastidious about the shape and colour of their flies than trout are."

Trout will eagerly take dead worms. Mr. Blakey says : "On one occasion we happened to have an old bait bag in our pocket, in which were twenty old, dried up, shrivelled worms, so dry indeed that they almost crumbled into powder between the finger and thumb. We steeped them in water, and contrived to thread them on a very small hook. The expedient proved successful ; and we returned home with a very fine basket of trout."

Salmon roe is a more seductive bait. The roe is used either as a paste or plain, as taken out of the fish, with a little salt sprinkled over it. This bait should be as large again as an ordinary horse-bean, and fastened upon the hook with a single fibre or two of common sheep's wool.

PERCH.

The perch is in good condition in August,
but will be better in September and October.
You may easily know the perch by the *spines* on
his back, and take care they do not run into your
hands if you happen to catch one. Many fish
for perch with a float, and this is good in lakes
or still water; but a paternoster is better —
that is, a bullet or heavy piece of lead at the end of
the line, allowed to touch the ground, and the hooks,
two or three, at intervals of a foot from each other
above the lead; hold the rod so that the line shall be
tight; you will then feel that peculiar bite of the
perch—twit, twit, twit, in rapid succession—so well-
known to the angler, and you may hook your fish,

and pull him out immediately. Where you take one, you may catch many more; they go in flocks. When a boy, we pulled up nearly twenty, as fast as we could drop the line in the same place.

The large red garden-worm, commonly called a lob, or dew-worm, is the best bait. Gather them, and put them in clean moss; pour a little milk over them—a smart blow will kill them—and then they are fit for use. You may also use fine shreds of lean raw beef or mutton, threaded upon the hook.

EEL.

He is found in all sorts of waters, ponds, lakes, ditches, trout-streams, canals, docks, and rivers. No water is too dirty for him and none too pure. He gets fat in mud, and where, apparently, there is nothing but stone. A fresh-water fish naturally, yet

he does not care if he gets into salt water. He goes
where he can get his dinner, and is not very nice as
to what it is From a dead crab to the leg of a live
duckling—he is by no means particular. When
cooked he is a most delicious fish, though some
persons can never touch eels ; "they look so much
like snakes." If hungry he will bite at almost
anything : he appears very fond of worms. The
best thing you can do is, when caught, to put your
foot upon him and cut off his head, or you will have
your line so tangled as to be unfit for use.

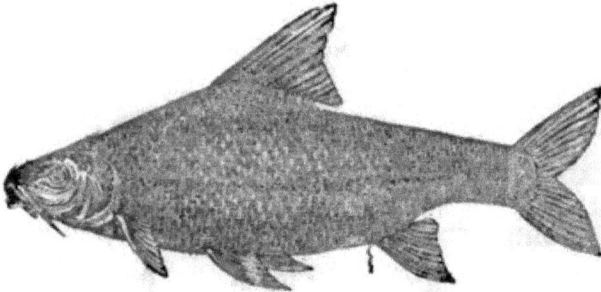

BARBEL.

So called from his *beard ;* the artist has only put
two—there are *four*. The barbel is a well-made,

handsome, powerful fish, very active and vigorous : mostly fond of rapid waters, near old walls or sunken timber. You must fish with the bait on the ground for barbel. The shot should be cased in sand-colored leather a foot or two above the hook. Tallow, greaves, and *bits of cheese* are the best bait. Keep the cheese in wet linen a day or two before using it to make it tough.

ROACH.

So called from the red in his eyes, and on his fins. You will almost always find many of them together. They are in season in August, and may be taken for the next two or three months. They like to swim in clear water ; but their flesh has a very muddy taste— not good for much.

You must not expect to catch roach in clear water,

unless your tackle be very fine and you keep out of
sight. You may catch roach with *flies*, artificial or
dead natural ones, at any part of the day. A good
plan is to kill the flies and dry them in an oven.
Put them on the hook and stand behind a bush or
tree ; drop the fly lightly on the top of the water.
The roach will think the fly has fallen from the tree
—will rise from his deep hole, and swim softly round
and round, and at last a good splash will tell you the
fish is hooked. If a large one you ought to let the
line run, and be careful how you land him or he will
be *sure* to break your line.

DACE.

Not much unlike the roach : but it is longer and
not so broad. The same tackle as used for the roach
will take the dace. A fly for the top of the water,

and a worm for the bottom. Dace are seldom found
except in rapid running water, where you may make
sure of him on a fine summer's evening, for he bites
freely.

CARP.

The carp is a very handsome fish, very shy, cun-
ning, and suspicious. They grow to a great size, live
to a great age, and are esteemed a great delicacy.
They may be caught in full condition at the end
of the summer. The carp may be carried in fresh
grass long journeys, if dipped in the water for a few
minutes every twenty-four hours; in this way they
are sent to different parts of the country, to stock
waters, and they thrive well after the journey.

Pastes of all kinds, beans and corn, are recommended as the best baits for carp. Grains of wheat, steeped in water till the skin bursts, are very good. A blue-bottle fly will be sure to take him if your tackle be fine.

TENCH.

A beautiful, thick fish, greenish or purplish yellow colour; found in lakes, ponds, and weedy rivers. These fish, like the last, may be carried long journeys in wet grass, without the slightest fear of their dying. The same bait as for carp—it must always touch the ground. He is some time before he swallows the bait, have patience, therefore, and when hooked, take care he does not run into the mud, or it will be very difficult to get him out again. From June to September, and even later, they may be caught.

BREAM.

Not a very beautiful fish, but very strong—and if
left alone, will grow to a great size; he has then
been compared to a large pair of bellows, and much
the same in flavour. As we have never tasted bellows, we cannot vouch for the correctness of this
opinion. A most remarkable thing is, that the
bream, if taken out of the water in very cold
weather, and wrapped in snow, with a piece of bread
steeped in alcohol put into his mouth, may be sent
a long journey without any injury to his health.
This is often done on the continent; perhaps he
would go as well if he were allowed to travel as a

teetotaller. He is very crafty, and the moment he is hooked, makes way for the weeds. Fish for him from August to October; let the bait touch the ground—the moment he bites the hook, land him, and then, if you can help it, don't touch him, his skin is so nasty.

GRAYLING.

Not much unlike the salmon-fry. They are found in streams with a sandy and stony bottom; are to be taken from September to November. Have the hook fine, and a running line—bait, worms, or gentles. When hooked, be carefully gentle, or you will lose your fish.

BLEAK.

There are prodigious numbers of them in the Caspian Sea; that is much too far to go for them, and you need not travel so far to take them, for they abound in all the fresh waters and rivers of Europe.

The tackle should be as light as possible. Take your stand by the side of a running or rushing stream; drop in your line, with three or four hooks on one line if you like. Bait the hooks with an artificial fly, tipped with a little bit of white leather or with gentles, and you may pull them out as fast as you like. It is said this fish affords the best sport to the young angler.

CHUB.

A strong, well-built fish, but not worth catching : found in most of the rivers in England, haunting old walls and deep, quiet holes. You may sometimes see them basking on the surface of the water over some deep hole. Tallow and cheese will make a good bait, or he may be caught with cherries.

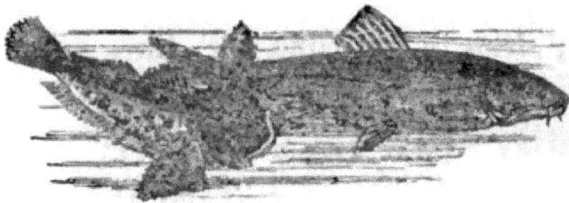

MILLER'S THUMB AND GUDGEON.

The miller's thumb is an odd little fellow, which you may catch in brooks. The gudgeon is worthy

of much more consideration; for it is a beautiful
and delicious fish, affording great amusement to the
young angler, and not difficult to catch. August and
September are the best months to take him. The
line should be all gut, with very small hooks, each
baited with a worm. Don't use a float, but fasten
a small bullet to the end of the line; let that just
touch the bottom, and you will feel the little short
jerks which indicate that the fish is tugging at the
bait, or is hooked, when, not in a hurry, you draw
out the litttle captive, and fill your basket in a very
short time.

POPE.

You will find him in *deep* water, with *mud* at the
bottom. You may fish with a quill float. The pope

is not a very great favourite of ours, we shall say no more about him.

STICKLEBACK.

MINNOW.

About both of which, and the way to catch them it is very probable you know more than we can tell you.

COAST FISHING.

On this subject nothing will be found in the preceding pages, we therefore insert a few remarks upon it here.

To fish in the salt water, a boat is required in nearly all places. This may be hired by the hour, the day, or the week. If you take a man or boy with you to manage the boat, he will "pull" you to the fishing-ground and tell you the right sort of bait. The fishing-ground will probably be a reef of rocks twenty or thirty feet under water, covered with sea-weed. On these are found large numbers of little living things which the fish feed upon. The fishing-ground is in fact the feeding-ground. You will require no rod for this sort of coast-fishing. A fishing line with a heavy piece of lead as a "sink," and two pieces of stick or whalebone called "chopsticks," made fast to the line about a foot from the ground with hooks at the end, will be sufficient. You may sit in the stern of the boat, and drop a line over each side. Hold the line between your finger and thumb, and you will feel instantly there is a bite; then haul away, and you will catch them, if they are in a biting humour, as fast as you can bait your hooks and haul in your fish. This is the way to catch whiting-pout.

Or you may let your boat drift with the tide along the coast, and catch codlings or gurnets. A slice of the end of the tail is the best bait. To get this slice, cut half way through to the bone, and then with the knife level with the bone, cut to the end of the tail.

A boat moored at the mouth of a small river just before it enters the sea, will be sure to supply you with some fish. Eels, flat fish, mullet, &c.

You perhaps are not aware that the salmon is a salt *and* fresh water fish.

It has been well said by the *Times*—" Salmon flock of their own accord to the rivers of these islands, and there deposit their spawn. The spawn is quickened into life, and myriads of little fish soon swarm in the stream.

At the beginning of May, or about this very time of the year, these young fish swim down the river to the open sea. There, in their natural feeding-grounds, they fatten so rapidly, that they increase, upon an average, at the rate of two or three pounds in weight every twelve months. The little fish, about the size of a gudgeon, which left the river in May, 1861, would be a fine salmon of six or seven pounds in April, 1863. But the singular point of the case is, that after fattening himself in this manner, he will, of his own free choice, come back again to be killed. The same instinct which took him off to sea, brings him back again to the river. He will infallibly return from his pasture to his nursery, and there offer himself for capture, without any cost for keep, attendance, or transport. He will make flesh more rapidly than an Essex pig, and do it all for nothing. The only thing he asks is not to be interrupted; not to be stopped when he comes here to breed; not to be turned back when he goes away to grow. All the rest he will do for himself; and will add pound after pound to his own substance for our benefit and delectation, if we will but leave him alone to do it.

"The explanation of the case, such as it is, is contained in its history. The salmon lives at sea, but comes up the rivers to spawn. The young salmon, bred in the river, go down to the sea to grow, after which they, in their turn, come up the river, as their parents did before them. They may therefore be caught either in the sea itself just by the river's mouth, or at any point of the river between its mouth and the place to which they ascend."

What a catch it would be to pull up a fine young salmon!

We hope to see the day when Young England will take salmon plentifully; but, if this be done, greater attention must be paid to the state of our rivers, and no fish must be taken either when they are about to spawn, or when they are very young. The tide nets stretched on stakes along on the shore near the mouth of rivers, which are covered at high water, are dreadfully destructive to salmon, they ought to be forbidden.

www.ingramcontent.com/pod-product-compliance
Lightning Source LLC
Chambersburg PA
CBHW021457090426
42739CB00009B/1767